A Season of Breakthrough

Four Strategies to Living a Life of Sustained Freedom

Paula Friedrichsen

International Standard Book Number: 0-96775-088-1

Library of Congress Cataloging-in-Publication Data
Friedrichsen, Paula.
A Season of Breakthrough; Four Strategies to Living a Life of Sustained Freedom
2012915385

Endorsements

"Every now and then you read a book of manifested truth and activated revelation that causes you to understand that the realities of Christ and HIS Word are not only possible, but accessible. At that moment, you feel the freedom to believe, and you run toward the destiny you did not have strength to receive before. This is one of those books and you are entering one of those moments. In 'A Season of Breakthrough; Four Strategies to Living a Life of Sustained Freedom' Paula Friedrichsen has successfully captured strategies from Heaven, timing from the heart of GOD, an understanding of pain that is unique, and a humorous insightful view that will aid anyone in trouble or transition to become an overcomer of magnificent proportions. Read it all, meditate on every section, talk about it with friends and watch GOD bring freedom and grace into the world you dwell within."

Rev. Michael Dalton, Yes Ministries International

"A breakthrough does not just come along, it takes courage, faith, and taking a stand. The strategies and lessons in 'A Season of Breakthrough' are not theory. They have been walked out through 1,000 days of pain, as Paula Friedrichsen learned what it takes to obtain and sustain freedom. From standing up to bullies, finding courage in the trenches, to breaking through to freedom—and keeping it—these strategies will enable anyone one to develop tenacious faith and walk in the fullness of what God has for their lives!"

Karen Power, Owner, Christian Speakers Services

Dedication

To Jim DeGolyer,
Friend, mentor, and passionate lover of God.

Contents

Acknowledgments

First and foremost, I would like to thank my dear friend, and first draft editor, Peggy Stovesand. I'm grateful for the many hours she invested in the editing of my manuscript.

I would also like to thank my husband Jeff for his support during this writing project. I'm blessed with a steady, loving, and kind husband who gives me "room to write."

I'd like to acknowledge the invaluable help of my daughter Amy. She freely offered her time, insight, and wisdom as I wrote—often helping me to verbally illustrate difficult concepts.

I'm grateful to my "final draft readers", and for the instruction, edits, opinions, and corrections they suggested as they read through my manuscript.

Lastly, I'd like to thank the leadership team at *Church on the Mountain*, in Crowley Lake, California. What a wonderfully motivating bunch they are! I'm extraordinarily thankful for their love, encouragement, and belief in me.

CHAPTER I

THE FACE OFF

One day, while enjoying an early morning walk through my neighborhood, I encountered a very large, very angry German shepherd. I was simply minding my own business, taking the same walk I'd taken a hundred times before, when all of a sudden this crazy-looking dog appeared out of nowhere forcing me into a face-off in the middle of the street. I froze in fear as he crouched low to the ground and crept toward me. His lips were curled, his teeth bared, and a low guttural growl accompanied his movement. I frantically looked up and down the street for an owner, but the neighborhood was deserted.

At this point my mind was filled with disturbing images of oozing blood, an ambulance ride, multiple surgeries, fighting for my life, a sorrowful funeral, and my children growing up motherless. I actually began to imagine just how much that first bite was going to hurt, and I recoiled in fear. On the outside I was doing my best to look unruffled and calm (I read once that a dog can sense fear, so I was trying to fake him out), but on the inside I was screaming like a four year old child.

Suddenly, something akin to indignation rose up in me and I thought, "*This is my neighborhood!*" I was outraged! I couldn't believe the audacity of that crazy dog to think he was going to attack and maul me on my own street, in my own neighborhood. Courage rolled up from my belly, I jerked my shoulders back, charged forward a step or two, pointed a rigid finger at him, and yelled, "*BACK OFF!*"

Like a sullen bully he slowly began to back up. When he was a safe distance away (because now *I* was the aggressor), he turned his back to me, and staying low to the ground, made his way out of my neighborhood.

I learned a few important lessons that day; the most important being, I have authority in *my neighborhood.*

Take a Stand

We must recognize our sphere of authority and take a stand. Our faith is encouraged and ignited in the act of subduing our enemies, and courage is built and refined when we are forced to face-off with demonic bullies. Courage is a God-attribute and Satan is incapable of possessing it. He is a bully, and at the heart of every bully is bravado and bluster—not courage. A bully becomes more powerful when he has persuaded his prey that he has the authority to steal, torment, and afflict. But thankfully, the final authority on every matter comes from the Word of God, and not the lies of the enemy. What does the Bible have to say about Satan's authority to steal, kill, and destroy?

"*The thief comes only to steal and kill and destroy; I came that they may have life, and have it abundantly.*" John 10:10

"*I have given you authority to trample on snakes and scorpions and to overcome all the power of the enemy; nothing will harm you.*" Luke 10:19

We can rest assured that the God of heaven and earth backs us up when we take our stand against the enemy. It is God's intention that we walk in sustained breakthrough and enjoy our victories in *fullness*.

The Victim Pitfall

If I had seen myself as a victim—running in terror from the German shepherd that day—you can be sure I would have been chased, caught, and bitten. The act of running would have drained me of my courage, and Fido would have gained confidence from my fear. However, in order to fully tap into our faith and courage we need to resist the temptation to see ourselves as victims of our circumstances. I was powerless and terrified as long as I saw myself as a victim of that crazed dog. *My salvation actually began with my outrage.* A sense of indignation and outrage must rise up in you when you're attacked. You may be *feeling* terrified, but the truth is that you are not a victim. You are not frail, or emotionally fragile, or pitiful, or weak. You are a child of God and you have every right and authority to protect your "neighborhood". Do not run. Stay and fight for the breakthroughs God has for you. They're *your* breakthroughs! That is *your* healing God began in your body; *your* restoration God began in your marriage; *your* grandchild who is returning to God; *your* mental freedom and clarity God is restoring to you; *your* finances God has begun to return; *your* addiction God is healing.

It won't necessarily be easy to face-off with demonic bullies—but it is thrilling when you see the victory!

Notes

Chapter 2

A Thousand Days of Pain

Several years ago I went through a difficult season, which at the time seemed overwhelming and insurmountable. Nothing I had experienced in my life, up until then, had prepared me for the level of pain and bondage that I found myself in. Yet the lessons, breakthroughs, strengths, and strategies I gained during that time period are invaluable to me now! I tell you this so you can know I'm sharing lessons in this book which were hard-won for me.... lessons which came out of deep places of suffering.

Part I – Breaking Through

Courage is formed in the trenches. I know this because I lived in a "trench" for three years.

On a sunny day in 2008 I woke up with my first migraine headache—and I had it (in one form or another) every day for the next 1000 days. Three years of acute pain, of medical tests, and of medications. Three years of panic, fear, and tears. Three years of prayer, deep worship, and a longing to be well.

For the first six weeks of this nightmare, my vision was extraordinarily sensitive. I couldn't look at our TV screen because the light and visual effects caused extreme pain. I had to cover the television with a blanket and be content to lie on the couch and listen to the sound. I couldn't look at my computer screen for the same reason. I couldn't read a book without completely exacerbating the pain, causing dizziness and a seasick feeling. I wore my sunglasses inside the house at all times, and didn't drive at night because the lights of oncoming cars caused me stabbing pain.

Things improved slowly, but for over a year and a half a sudden shift in lighting or abrupt loud noise could set off an explosive round of migraine pain and extreme nausea. I remember a time when my husband accidentally banged into the bedroom door while coming to bed late one night. This loud, unexpected sound set off a four-week cycle of vicious throbbing in my right temple. Throughout this time in my life there was nothing but pain—and my obsession to get out of pain.

Because I'm a proactive kind of person I tried everything I could think of to get better. I took almost every drug my neurologist suggested. I tried many holistic methods to bring healing. I ate organic foods, drank purified water, and cut most of the sugar out of my diet. I taped healing Scriptures on my bathroom mirror and I read them aloud every day. I requested prayer at my church at every opportunity. Basically, I was on a mission to be healed.

Simultaneously, during this time period I was taking more and more narcotic pain medications in an effort to get a few hours of relief. Most nights I would creep out of bed in the middle of the night to take one pill or another—then struggle to go back to sleep oppressed with the weight of guilt for taking so many meds. It was a vicious cycle, which added greatly to my overall misery and fear. During this time I cried out to God for deliverance, and pressed into Him in deeper ways.

One of the most important steps I took in my journey was to keep my mouth shut. I refused to complain (with very few exceptions). I had a deep knowing in my heart that it was of vital importance that I not speak negatively about my situation. Certainly I had times of pouring out all my fears and frustrations with the people who love me—but for the most part, I kept silent and put my trust in God. And when I speak of "trust in God" I mean a deep, stoic, anchor-like trust…. a trust that only God could develop in me.

At some point this deep trust gave birth to courage. Courage to stand uncompromisingly on God's promises of healing found in His Word, in spite of the terrorizing amounts of pain. Courage to put my roots of faith deep into God's Presence, allowing nothing to steal my peace and joy in the midst of suffering. I began to see myself as a strong oak tree, with roots that went down deep into the soil of God's Word. As each new wind of migraine pain would blow against me, threatening to topple my faith, my roots would grab hold of God's promises and I would stand strong.

God began to move drastically in my situation about two and half years into the illness. First, He brought me a tremendous increase of comfort, accountability, and anointed prayer through my leadership team at church. Then, He brought a wonderful minister named Jim DeGolyer to our church for a month. During that time I had the opportunity to meet with Jim and his wife Mary, and God greatly expanded my understanding and experience of His Presence (more about this in chapters 9 and 10).

Three years after my headache trial began, almost to the day, I woke up excited and cheerful. You see, that was the day I was to be ordained by our church fathers. That morning I awoke with severe migraine pain in my left temple, which, quite honestly, had become my new normal. As I lay there I did my usual self-assessment to see how bad I felt. And it was at that moment the Lord spoke clearly to me and said, "*No longer will any and every activity or stress have the power to give you a headache.*"

Breakthrough had finally come!

The morning of my ordination marked the day I was released from the ongoing nightmare of migraine headaches and I began to dramatically improve.

Part 2 – Sustained Freedom

While the morning of my ordination marked the day I was released from the vice-grip of migraines, it also marked the first day of my journey to walk in *sustained* breakthrough and freedom. God had brought His power and His word to my situation, now it was my turn to walk it out. Many times after God works miraculously in our lives the enemy will do his best to steal that victory. Satan doesn't just shrug his shoulders and say, "*Well, the jig is up boys, let's vacate the premises.*" No, it doesn't always work that way. When God brings breakthrough, sometimes there will be a "contest" over it. And there was certainly a contest over my healing!

The resulting strategies I learned during that season of life are like planks in a foot bridge. Each plank took me closer to a life of sustained breakthrough until I reached the other side and could say with confidence, "*With God's help I'll never go back to that pain or bondage again.*"

And actually, I learned several of these life-changing strategies over fifteen years ago when God dramatically healed me of Lyme disease. It was then that the Lord first began to teach me how to stand on my healing with bulldog tenacity. Teaching others to walk in the fullness of what God has accomplished in their lives has become a passion of mine. I long to help people receive their breakthrough from God, and develop tenacious faith to hold on to and fully enjoy sustained freedom!

Lord of the Breakthrough!

God has a history of breakthrough in my life, and I'm sure the same can be said for your life as well. Jesus has tremendous credibility with me based on a whole life of loving me, talking to me, healing me, rescuing me, and leading me. His credibility only grows as I see His amazing work in the lives of my family and friends. Add to that all the people we read about in the Bible, and I'm sold! Jesus has "street cred" with me, and I'll follow Him anywhere.

If you've read Psalms, Chronicles, or the books of Samuel, then you know that King David was passionate about his love and allegiance to God. He had an intimate, authentic walk with God and experienced major breakthroughs in the many years he lived upon the earth. In fact, it was one of David's victories where we first learn an important name of God: *Baal Perazim*, which means, "Lord of the Breakthrough" or "The God Who Bursts Through."

In 2 Samuel 5, we read that, after years of waiting, hiding, and being hunted by King Saul, David finally became king over all Israel. David had just experienced his most profound breakthrough up to that point in his life, and as the story unfolds we find him reigning in the City of David in blessing and abundance. Here's what happens next:

When the Philistines heard that David had been anointed king over Israel, they went up in full force to search for him, but David heard about it and went down to the stronghold. Now the Philistines had come and spread out in the Valley of Rephaim; so David inquired of the Lord, "Shall I go and attack the Philistines? Will you deliver them into my hands?"

The Lord answered him, "Go, for I will surely deliver the Philistines into your hands."

So David went to Baal Perazim, and there he defeated them. He said, "As waters break out, the Lord has broken out against my enemies before me." So that place was called Baal Perazim.

We serve a God of ever increasing breakthrough! He desires to build upon the testimonies in our lives, to bring us into greater and greater freedom. He uses His Word to build faith and credibility—but He also uses our past victories to build upon. Then as we look back on our past victories we gain assurance that God is working in our current situation.

I'm sure when David heard about the Philistines coming to attack Israel, in "full force", he wasn't necessarily happy about that report. However, I'm also sure it provoked memories of past victories which sustained his confidence in

God's ability to see him through his present crisis. In the end, David and the Israelite army prevailed!

I also find it noteworthy that it was *just after* David finally entered into the fullness of what God had promised him (kingship over Israel) the enemy came against him in "full force". This is a pattern we see played out over and over again in Scripture and in our lives today. Demonic interest is always sparked when we begin to take new ground, go forward, and walk in freedom. However, instead of being intimidated and frightened by this kind of attack, we need to see it as an indicator that we're on the right track and proceed "without" caution. If God has declared breakthrough over us, then we can boldly go forward despite the onslaught our actions may have provoked. The Lord won't direct us to take new ground without backing us up. He's not going to leave us hanging. He absolutely, positively will come through for us, just as He came through for David when the Philistines came against Israel.

Another example of this scenario is seen in Exodus, chapters 4 and 5. Let's pick up the story just after the Israelite elders have met with Moses and Aaron to hear the good news that God is going to deliver them from slavery. We read, "*When they heard that the Lord was concerned about them and had seen their misery, they bowed down and worshiped.*"

It's obvious from their response that the Israelites truly believed the word of the Lord. How exciting it must have been to finally see light at the end of the tunnel after 400 years of slavery! At this point they were probably beginning to imagine what life might be like as free men and woman!

Yet, just a few paragraphs later we see their hopes dashed as Pharaoh viciously retaliates against them after being approached by Moses and asked to allow the Israelites to go worship God in the desert. In fact, according to Exodus 5:6, Pharaoh's retaliation came *the very same day* that Moses and Aaron gave him God's message to "*let my people go*."

Before Moses and Aaron were out the door Pharaoh had given orders to increase the Israelite's bondage, as retaliation for their audacious belief that they could be free.

Pharaoh must have thought, "*How dare they! They are slaves, not free men. How dare they presume to even imagine themselves free. They are mine! They are my slaves, my captives, my prisoners. They will never be free!*"

While Moses and Aaron weren't put off by Pharaoh's bravado, the Israelites certainly were. In verse 19 they said to Moses, "*May the Lord look upon you and judge you! You have made us a stench to Pharaoh and his officials and have put a sword in their hand to kill us.*"

It saddens me that we so often become discouraged and turn back at the first sign of opposition. Instead of understanding that most victories are going to take tenacious faith, ongoing counsel from the Holy Spirit, courage, time, effort, and repentance—we think something silly like, "*Well, it must not be God's timing for me to be free.*" The very fact that the enemy has risen up to oppose you as you begin to take steps toward freedom is the tip-off that you're on the right track. Keep going! Thankfully Moses did keep going, and his bold actions brought an end to the captivity of God's people.

The Pitfall of Comparison

My husband, Jeff, is twenty years older than I am. And because he already had grown children by the time we married, we agreed to only have one child. But as that sweet-smelling little bundle of joy was laid in my arms, I knew that one baby was not going to be enough for me! So I did what I have always done when I had a problem or an unmet desire: I took it to God in prayer. One day He answered me, letting me know that He did indeed have another baby for us. But, He told me not to pester my husband about it since Jeff felt strongly about us having only one child. God wanted me to wait on Him and His timing, and to leave my desire in His hands.

So…. I waited. And waited. And waited. I prayed, and waited, prayed and waited—and waited some more.

Around the same time a girlfriend of mine expressed her strong desire for a baby too. She was having trouble conceiving—yet both she and her husband badly wanted children. Year after year my friend would hope to get pregnant, but it never happened. Meanwhile, I was also waiting on God to bring me my promised baby by changing Jeff's heart on the matter.

Seven years into my "journey of waiting" God turned my situation around and gave me the sweetest little baby girl you've ever seen. However, if I had had my eyes on my friend's lack of breakthrough, I may have missed mine. It's easy to compare our lives to others and become discouraged by lack of answered prayer. But really, the only thing you need to know is that God has been faithful to *you*. He has credibility in *your* life. Your job is to walk in fellowship with Him, not with your doubts. Base your expectations of God on your past breakthroughs and on His Word to you—not on the (seeming) lack of breakthrough of others.

Your healing is not dependant upon whether your friend received healing. Your financial breakthrough is not based upon whether your family member experienced breakthrough. Your marriage restoration is not based upon whether your sister or brother experienced restoration. If you base your expectations on what has transpired in the lives of those around you, you may end up disappointed. God has credibility in *your* life and He has spoken specific promises to *you*. That is enough.

* * * *

In the following chapters we're going to be talking about four strategies to obtaining and living a life of sustained breakthrough: 1) *Risky Obedience* 2) *Tenacious Faith* 3) *Destiny Awareness* and 4) *Transforming Love*. Put your spiritual walking shoes on and get ready to cross over into a new realm of abundance. God has so much more for you! Let's go there together.

Notes

CHAPTER 3

THE STRATEGY OF *RISKY OBEDIENCE*

The first strategy for entering into a season of breakthrough and living a life of sustained freedom involves learning to walk in obedience to the revealed will of God for your life. I'm not talking about "religious tightrope walking" or living in a constant state of navel gazing, perfectionism, or behavioral meticulousness. I'm talking about living in a state of supernatural grace to obey even the most difficult and risky things God asks you to do.

Walking in risky obedience will require you to rely upon the Holy Spirit for courage and resiliency. You'll gain momentum in your pursuit of obedience by the knowledge that the Lord always knows what is best for us. He can be completely trusted because He is a perfect, loving, and faithful Father. He will only make requests of us which will draw us closer to Him, and closer to enjoying the abundant life He promises us in His Word.

ONE IS TOO MANY AND A THOUSAND IS NEVER ENOUGH

Several months before the miraculous breakthrough of my migraine headache illness, the Holy Spirit instructed me to stop taking my prescribed painkiller, Vicodin. This was a defining moment for me, and one which filled me with dread. I had tried unsuccessfully to stop taking Vicodin many times during the three year illness, but found I always slipped back into use when the pain became unmanageable. Each time that I would relapse back to Vicodin use, I would travel down a dark road which degenerated into compulsion and addiction (a common problem with narcotics). Basically, I found it impossible to successfully manage my pain medication use on my own.

There's an adage about addiction which says; "*One is too many, and a thousand is never enough*". That phrase perfectly describes what it's like to be dependant on painkillers. And for the sake of clarity let me say that I was dependant on narcotic painkillers because A) they are incredibly addictive, and most people who take them long-term become physically and psychologically dependant on them, and B) I was in *Pain*! Pain will make you do crazy things. Things which are out of character. Things you would normally never do.

During this time in my life I found myself between a rock and a hard place. I desired to stop taking the narcotics—but I was in massive amounts of pain. Yet, the truth of the matter was I was also taking painkillers when I was only in moderate pain. I began to play the game of "*How much pain am I in?*" I was constantly in a state of monitoring my pain level to assess if it was an appropriate time to take a pill. And let's just be honest here and admit there's a "payoff" for taking a pain pill; a euphoric high, which is the reason why narcotics are so addictive. (I do realize that some people do not experience a euphoric feeling from opiates). Long-term narcotic use is like a runaway train… once it has gained speed, it becomes difficult to stop.

Looking back, some of the creative and inventive ways I came up with to try and *manage* my Vicodin use seem almost comical to me now. Yet, at the time I was willing to do almost anything to outwit, outlast, and outplay addiction. But here's the thing: you can't outwit, outlast, or outplay addiction. Addiction wins every time.

But I tried… oh how I tried! Here are a few of the circus acts I performed hoping to stave off pain medication dependence:

- I kept the pills at the very back of the medicine cabinet under a towel, so I wouldn't "see" them. (Yeah, that worked…).
- I took the pills to my friend Jan's house so I wouldn't have them readily available. (This tactic only resulted in a deepened friendship with Jan, who I basically saw every single day for a year).
- I put a big, bold note on the pill bottle which said, "Excruciating Pain!" (But then went ahead and used them for moderate pain).
- I asked a friend to be an "accountability partner" and I promised to call her each time I was contemplating taking a pill so she could talk me out of it. (Which only made me despise and avoid her).
- At different points in my illness I flushed them down the toilet, threw them in the dumpster, and ground them up in the garbage disposal. (Only to find myself waiting at the pharmacy door at 7:59AM on the next available refill date).
- I obsessively counted my pills and *always* knew how many I had at any given time. I fixated over how to make the pills last until the next refill, and I was tormented by the thought that I would run out and have to endure the migraine pain without them.
- Every single night I would plan to "start fresh" in the morning. Like blowing a diet, I would beat myself up for that day's behavior, and promise myself that the next day would be different. (My "next day resolve" would usually last until 10:00AM when the pain began to dominate my day).
- I prayed about my Vicodin use constantly. Each night as I crawled into bed I would begin a long discourse with God. "*Oh Lord, I'm so sorry. Forgive me. Help*

me!" (One night as I was beginning my "pain med conversation" with God, I clearly heard the Holy Spirit say, "*Can we talk about 'anything' else tonight?*" That gave me a much needed laugh!)

- I would constantly obsess about ways to taper my Vicodin use. My thinking became compulsive, and I would spend hours thinking and mentally chasing my tail around and around—trying to figure out a way to stop taking painkillers addictively—without having to stop taking them completely. My thoughts went something like this: *How many pills did I take today…? Is the pain bad enough to take another…? Maybe I should wait… Maybe I should take a half a pill… When am I due for my next refill …? Do the girls at the pharmacy think I'm a drug addict…? What if I run out of pills…? Next time I'll only take a pill if the pain is unbearable…*

It was in the midst of this ludicrous pain-med cycle that God spoke clearly and distinctly, "*Stop taking the Vicodin completely.*" He confirmed His word through my pastor and leadership team at my church. They had been aware of my migraine illness, as well as my pain medication use (one of the things I did right during this trial was to surround myself with trustworthy friends, family, and prayer partners who knew of my struggles with migraine pain and with Vicodin. They prayed for me, counseled me, held me accountable, fought for me in prayer, and hung in there with me until I was free!).

At this point in my journey I was still in an absurd amount of daily pain. It would ebb and flow… spike and decline… but it was *always* there. As I pressed God for confirmation and clarity regarding His extraordinarily difficult request, He spoke the words "unreasonable sacrifice" to me. This phrase brought me tremendous comfort! God *knew* He was asking me to stop taking the one medication which actually greatly reduced the pain. He knew it would be difficult beyond what I could personally bear. He knew the demons of addiction and fear would be waiting for me on "day one" of my new journey—and that I would literally have to battle hell to get free. And yet, He still wanted me to do it. And so, with fear and trembling, I agreed. Because He is God, and because He is always good, I knew something wonderful and miraculous would surely follow His directive.

(As a side note; I'm certainly **not** saying that everyone who takes prescription pain medication is being disobedient to God. Not at all! I'm just stating that personally, I found it difficult to receive healing from God while I was still on narcotics. The simple reason was the "payoff" for being in pain. Many times, at the first sign of extreme migraine pain, I would actually feel a little thrill because I knew it meant I would be justified to increase my Vicodin use. So, even though the increase in pain would be distressing, could last for up to six weeks, and would bring my life to a relative standstill—the addictive qualities of the narcotic would provide a payoff for the pain. In reality, my spirit was willing to receive freedom and healing from God—but my flesh was an incorrigible tyrant who threw a tantrum every time I tried to deny it what it craved.)

I came across the following quote shortly before I began my journey to go pain-med free.

"*Until we make the decision that we will not go back, regardless of how painful it gets, we will not go forward with the force of faith that it will take to fulfill our destiny.*" -Rick Joyner

I taped that quote on my refrigerator and read it about a 1000 times a day. I also held tightly to this Scripture found in Jonah 2:8, "*Those who cling to worthless idols forfeit the grace that could be theirs.*" I hated the thought of "forfeiting" the very grace I needed to fight addiction and receive healing. I was ready to lay my idol down, once and for all.

Armed with God's clear directive, the support of my family and closest friends, and that anointed quote from Rick Joyner, I went off all pain meds cold turkey. *

During those first few days and weeks I battled extreme migraine pain, fear, insomnia, anxiety, and addiction.

I was shaky, nauseous, achy, and sicker than a dog. I endured each day the best I could, and I clung to God.

On the practical side, I emailed my neurologist and asked him to no longer prescribe painkillers of any kind to me. I called the pharmacy and canceled my prescription. I drank lots of purified water, ate healthy, and did everything I could to help my body detoxify from three years of drug use. Within a week of stopping the pain meds, God directed me to stop taking all sleeping pills, antacids, and laxatives, as well.

You see, in an effort to combat the side affects of the Vicodin, I had also become a voracious consumer of over-the-counter medications, and it was now time to stop the madness. This too seemed like a request that I would be unable to obey apart from God's intervention. I simply did not possess the strength to walk away from the relief that these medications brought me each day. To not have sleeping pills or Nyquil to look forward to at the end of a long day of migraine pain seemed unthinkable.

Yet, I knew God was speaking… so I obeyed. I provided the "willingness" and the Holy Spirit provided the supernatural strength. It's hard to explain, but while on one hand it was agony to resist the temptation to medicate myself with things like Vicodin and sleeping pills—on the other hand I was able to somehow endure, resist, and conquer because of the courage and grace God supplied me. It was difficult… but not impossible.

* **End Note:** For those dealing with narcotic addiction and dependency; I am not necessarily recommending the "cold turkey" method. You'll need to find out exactly what God is saying to *you* about your particular situation. You should also discuss your desire to get off pain medications with your doctor, a pain management professional, or a rehab center.

Notes

Chapter 4

Lessons About *Risky Obedience*

Lesson 1: You Are Not in Control. During this season of turmoil I learned that "trust" has to do with giving up control over my life and circumstances (as if I really had any in the first place!). For example, having no control… no way to get out of pain… no way to medicate, to soothe, and to "take the edge off" my pain was infuriating and disquieting, to say the least. It was like being dropped in choppy seas, and the out-of-control, fearful, seasick feeling I endured during that time reminded me of an incident which happened over ten years ago.

When our children were young, my husband and I took them kayaking in Hawaii. Our first challenge was to divvy up our kids so we were equally matched. My husband was paired with our eight-year old daughter in one kayak, and I was paired with our fifteen-year old son in the other.

The second challenge was dealing with the sea itself. Rather than cutting smoothly and swiftly through scenic glassy waters, as I had envisioned, we strained every muscle in our attempts to cut through extremely choppy seas. Though my son was only fifteen at the time, he was built like a tank, standing several inches taller then me and outweighing me by close to 100 pounds. So he was the perfect choice for the sturdy backseat position.

Our laid-back-to-a-fault, beach-bum kayak guide had instructed us that the backseat kayak occupant was to use his paddle to steer the kayak, while the front seat person was to paddle straight, without turning. This was important information because, once we paddled out to open sea, we discovered this trip would require constant steering and readjustment of our positions to avoid losing sight of our laid-back-beach-bum guide (who was a ½ mile in front of us, blithely cutting through huge swells, and merrily racing along without looking back).

Allowing my son Andrew to steer the kayak really shouldn't have been a problem, except that I refused to let go and allow him to take control. Because I was fearful in such choppy waters, I kept trying to steer our kayak and adjust our course, thinking I was in a better position to judge where we should be going. Consequently, my son and I were fighting each other with opposite moves and falling further and further behind the rest of the kayakers. In better circumstances I would have happily turned the steering over to him. It was when things got turbulent, upsetting, and our lives seemed in jeopardy, that I had trouble letting go of control. Andrew finally said to me in exasperation, "*Mom, unless you stop trying to steer, I can't do my job!*"

I struggled to trust him and let go, but when I finally did, things went far more smoothly. Andrew was much stronger then me and well able to perform the maneuvers needed to constantly correct the direction of our kayak in those choppy waters.

God desires to lead and direct you regarding specific choices and decisions for your life. Psalm 25:12 says, "*Who, then, are those who fear the Lord? He will instruct them in the ways they should choose.*" It's clear from that Scripture (and many like it) that God's best is for you to hear and obey His voice. Things gets dicey when your marriage is desperately unhappy—but God tells you not to get a divorce; or your job is causing you distress—but God tells you to hang in there; or you love your hometown—but God tells you to move; or you're in relentless pain—but God says to stop taking narcotic painkillers.

During my season of "risky obedience" I learned that I am not in control of my own life. I have willingly turned over the paddles to Jesus, and he's directing, choreographing, and maneuvering the kayak of my life. I also learned that He is stunningly faithful and gloriously trustworthy in all things. What He requires of us may be tremendously difficult at times, but He'll lead and guide us through every step until we arrive safely on the other side.

LESSON 2: LEARN TO STAND YOUR GROUND. We must learn the lesson that after God moves in our lives there will be a "contest" over our breakthrough. And because of that, we'll need to be trained to tenaciously stand in our new land of promise and refuse to leave… refuse to waver… and refuse to run.

Some people lose momentum if the pain returns, or the marriage gets hard again, or the adult child makes wrong choices again, or they get treated unfairly again. They begin to speak negatively, and all of a sudden it seems as though they are sliding down a slippery hill backwards. They wonder, "*How did I get here? How did I lose all the ground I had gained? I know God worked miraculously in my life—where did all that progress go? All the healing? All the restoration?*"

For me, standing my ground meant refusing to go back to narcotic pain medications. But it was much more than that: I was also learning to step into my promise of healing before it had completely manifested. I was learning to *act* well before I felt well… To smile when I really wanted to cry in panic and frustration…. To make the bed when I really wanted to crawl back in the bed…. To cook dinner for the family when I really wanted to take a pain pill, curl up in a ball under the dining room table, and refuse to live my life until the pain went away.

Cooking dinner was an act of warfare. Making the bed was an act of warfare. Smiling, laughing, hugging, and asking others about themselves were acts of warfare. Those actions showed the enemy, showed myself, showed my family, and showed God that I was refusing to go backwards. (Let me give a quick disclaimer here; I certainly realize there will be times in your "journey to breakthrough" that you *will* "shrink back in fear", or that you *will* be a puddle of tears, or that you *will* be unable to smile, laugh, hug, or persevere. I get that. I've been there. And God's grace, love, and mercy will cover you in those times. He's not looking for the strong and able—He's simply looking for those who will trust and obey Him regardless of their suffering.)

Allow your suffering to cultivate courage and the ability to "stand." Perseverance in the midst of suffering can be the perfect greenhouse to cultivate courage, when God is the gardener. Remember, He will never ask us to do something which we're incapable of doing. He only asks of us what He is willing to help us accomplish.

Below are several Scriptures to hold on to as you learn to stand your ground. Tape them on your refrigerator…memorize them…highlight them in your Bible…do whatever you have to do get them deep into your heart. They will be life, and hope, and an anchor in you. They will help you resist the temptation to tuck tail and run when the battle becomes fierce. But first, let's look at the definition of the word "stand" found in the Webster's dictionary:

Stand: "To face or encounter; to undergo or submit to; to endure without harm or damage or without giving way; to tolerate."

- "*Do not be afraid.* ***Stand firm*** *and you will see the deliverance the Lord will bring you…*" Exodus 14:13
- "*You will not have to fight this battle. Take up your positions;* ***stand firm*** *and see the deliverance the LORD will give you…*" 2 Chronicles 20:17
- "*He lifted me out of the slimy pit, out of the mud and mire; he set my feet on a rock and gave me a firm place to* ***stand****.*" Psalm 40:2
- "*Therefore, my dear brothers and sisters,* ***stand firm****. Let nothing move you. Always give yourselves fully to*

the work of the Lord, because you know that your labor in the Lord is not in vain." 1 Corinthians 15:58

- "*Be on your guard;* ***stand firm*** *in the faith; be courageous; be strong.*" 1 Corinthians 16:13

LESSON 3: OBEDIENCE PLAYS A PART IN DELIVERANCE. Let me start this point by clarifying what I'm *not* saying. I'm not saying that until you measure up and become a perfect son or daughter God will not heal or deliver you—as though you had to earn it. Jesus made a way for us to be saved, forgiven, delivered, and healed when *He* hung on the cross *for* us. I personally know of many folks who have received deliverance from God regardless of their obedience to His revealed will for their lives. We don't receive deliverance from God because *we* are good, but because *He* is good!

So, while it's true that we receive His gift of deliverance and healing freely—we may also need to stay in step with the Holy Spirit, so that we can continue to walk in the freedom and joy He died to give us. And staying in step with the Holy Spirit means obeying His directives and commands, whether general (found in the Bible) or personal (like his directive to me regarding pain meds).

There's Scripture found in 1 John 3:21, 22 & 24 which will help illuminate this point: "*Dear friends, if our hearts do not condemn us, we have confidence before God and receive from him anything we ask, because we keep His commands and do what pleases Him... The one who keeps God's commands lives in Him, and He in them. And this is how we know that he lives in us: We know it by the Spirit He gave us.*"

You can find a key to breakthrough in the Scripture above! The key is—"*if your heart does not condemn you*", you will have confidence before God and receive from Him anything you ask of Him." Some people are trying to "stand in faith" for a promise from God, but their heart is condemning them every time they do what God has told them specifically *not* to do.

We also see this principle in 1 Timothy 1:18-19, "*Timothy, my son, I give you this instruction in keeping with the prophecies once made about you, so that by following them you may fight the good fight,* ***holding on to faith and a good conscience****. Some have rejected these and so have shipwrecked their faith.*"

If I had found myself unwilling to go to that place of trust and obedience with God, I may have found it difficult to receive healing. Why? Because, I had gotten to the point where my heart was condemning me each time I would take the pain pills. Persisting in my disobedience would have "shipwrecked my faith".

Although God is full of compassion and loving-kindness when we're going through difficult trials in life, the truth is that being pitiful and pathetic doesn't move God's hand. Crying under a "quilt of self pity" on the couch for days at a time doesn't move God's hand. Faith moves God's hand! We see in Hebrews 11:6 that, "*without faith it is impossible to please God, because anyone who comes to him must believe that he exists and that he rewards those who earnestly seek him.*" And in Hebrews 10:38-39 we read, "*But my righteous one will live by faith. And I take no pleasure in the one who shrinks back. But we do not belong to those who shrink back and are destroyed, but to those who have faith and are saved.*"

It takes faith to obey God! When God requires risky obedience from us, He doesn't expect us to do it alone. He simply asks us to trust Him, obey Him, and walk in faith. He'll do the rest. Just begin. Take a step. See what God will do!

You might be wondering exactly what Risky Obedience looks like. It looks like this:

- Abraham was asked by God to sacrifice his only son Isaac. Now, the Lord had already prophesied an entire race would come from the loins of Isaac—yet God "unreasonably" requested that Abraham go up to mount Moriah and slay him. With no assurance of Isaac's safety, except God's prior prophetic word to him, Abraham obeyed. In the end, God spared Isaac, provided a ram for the sacrifice, and completely fulfilled His word to Abraham in the years to come. (Genesis 22)

- Moses was required by God to stride into Pharaoh's palace and demand the release of the entire population of Hebrew slaves. If he failed, his likely future would be death at the hands of his own people. With no guarantees, except the Word of the Lord, Moses obeyed. And the Hebrew nation was gloriously and miraculously freed from bondage! (Exodus 3-13)
- Gideon was required by God to become the captain of the Israeli army and free his nation from the ongoing pillaging of the Midianites. Gideon had no formal military training and was not a leader in his community. If he failed, he would likely face death. Yet God asked him to take charge and go to war based solely on the Word of the Lord. Gideon obeyed, and in the end, Israel annihilated their enemy. (Judges 7)
- Joshua and the Israelite army were told by God to march around Jericho seven times to conquer it. This seemed unreasonable, ridiculous, and foolish. If they failed, the Israelites would be a laughing stock and in jeopardy of obliteration by the surrounding nations. Joshua had no guarantee it would work, except for the Word of the Lord. Joshua obeyed, and the walls of Jericho fell! (Joshua 6)
- Blind Bartimaeus threw off his beggar's cloak (the garment which distinguished him as handicapped and secured his only source of income… begging) and ran to Jesus to be healed. Had he stayed in his comfort zone where he was at ease and known—he wouldn't have received his sight. He had to take action, and he did! First, he acted upon the urge to shout out to Jesus, despite the harsh and negative opinions of those around him. Then he fired up enough faith to throw off his beggar's cloak and sprint over to the Lord. And

lastly, he confidently asked Jesus for what he wanted; "*I want to see.*" Jesus healed him! Bartimaeus had a radical encounter with the healing Jesus. (Mark 10)

Obedience can play a role in deliverance. It's not a case of you "trying to be good enough" to earn breakthrough from God. It's a case of you walking in the fear of the Lord and "doing life" the way He tells us to. Whatever risky obedience God has been requiring from you—He will come along side to help you accomplish it. Nothing is impossible with God and no promise is too big for Him to fulfill. Be like blind Bartimaeus and thumb your nose at the criticisms and negativity of those around you, throw off your old persona of failure or victimhood, and press into God like never before. He will always back up His Word. Even if you have *nothing* but the Word of the Lord as your guarantee—it is enough. Even if you've tried many times before and failed, go for it again. If He came through for Abraham, Moses, Joshua, Gideon, and Bartimaeus, He'll come through for you.

Lesson 4: God's Timing is Important. Staying in sync with God's timing for your life is essential, and obedience plays a role. God has a specific, wonderful, fulfilling plan for your life, which is why staying in step with the Holy Spirit is so vital.

Now, that doesn't mean you're on a tightrope when it comes to the Holy Spirit…one wrong move and your destiny plummets to the ground with a splat. But rather, that you're engaged in an affectionate, intimate, trusting friendship with God—where you're doing your part to hear and obey His voice—and He's doing His part to lovingly help you along the way.

We can see God's faithfulness to accomplish the prophetic words spoken over Jesus' life in the book of Matthew. Over and over again, we read something to the effect of, "*All this took place to fulfill what the Lord had said through the prophet…*" or "*But this has all taken place that the writings of the prophets might be fulfilled.*" God was intrinsically and intricately committed to fulfilling His Word in the life of Jesus, and He is committed to fulfilling His Word in your life as well. However, it means you'll have to be willing to face conflict or discomfort at times, in order to stay in step with God's timing, and to see His prophetic words fulfilled in your life.

As we watch the life of Jesus in the gospels we see that Jesus obeyed even to the point of dying on a cross. Hebrews 12:2 says, "*And let us run with perseverance the race marked out for us, fixing our eyes on Jesus, the pioneer and perfecter of faith. For the joy set before him he endured the cross, scorning its shame, and sat down at the right hand of the throne of God.*" Jesus had a prophetic mindset. He went through the traumatic and painful suffering on the cross—because He had confidence in His promised future joy. Jesus is an example and forerunner for us, and He promises to help us along our way.

It is a normal human behavior to avoid discomfort and distress. But some people have taken it to a whole new level by making "pain avoidance" a fulltime job. Which of course only leads to more pain, distress, discomfort, and confusion.

For example, if we avoid unpleasant things to the point where we aren't taking care of business, we will invariably miss out on God's timing for the next chapter of our lives. It's possible for us to miss our breakthroughs if we're obsessed with avoiding anything unpleasant, painful, arduous, or exhausting. Here are a few examples:

- Many people are waiting for a miracle in their marriage, but they avoid conflict at all costs. Because conflict is painful, scary, and unsettling—they continue to swallow their grievances and disappointments instead of working through them with their partner. They want a healed and restored marriage but they won't "pass through the pain to get to the promise."

- Many people desire to be healed. For some it will be as simple as asking and receiving from God. For others, God has spoken to them about an area of disobedience that needs to be rectified. They find themselves stuck in the quagmire of "God has spoken to me to obey Him in such and such. I continue to disobey. My heart condemns me each time I disobey. And I find myself unable to receive from God" (1 John 3:21).
- Many people long for a healthy, fit body. God has given them specific directions to begin the journey toward vibrant good health—but each time they begin the process of sugar withdrawal, sore muscles, hunger pains, or self-denial, they go back to the old ways and say things like, "*I'll start again tomorrow*." or "*This is way too hard, I must have missed God*."
- Many people are called to write a book, start a ministry, open a new business, etc. They have inspired ideas, and the creativity needed to begin their new endeavor. They want to begin. They intend to begin. God told them to begin. They pray about beginning. However, they never give themselves over to the arduous process of actually beginning their new venture.

God has a breakthrough, a future, and a new chapter for you! For some of you, your new start may actually be *hinged* upon your obedience. If you identify with that last sentence, then let me encourage you: the Holy Spirit continually spoke to me as I struggled to walk out of pain medication dependency, "*Keep going, Paula, it will be worth it*." I was also deeply encouraged by this compelling quote by Christian speaker Jonathan Welton, "*Physical acts of obedience, done in faith, release spiritual realities*." Both of these statements proved true for me. It truly was well worth it to do things God's way! And my "physical act of obedience, done in faith", released me from the bondage of addiction and released the "spiritual reality" of healing in my life.

It doesn't matter how many times you've failed in your attempts to obey God in a particularly hard directive—today is a new day. And really, it's more than a new day—it's *your* new day! It's your fresh start! You can start that fitness regime God spoke to you about today. You can start writing your book today. You can begin to step out into ministry today. Today you can start the journey of getting off prescription painkillers, or quitting smoking, or reducing or stopping your alcohol intake. You can walk away from that illicit affair today. You can take steps toward becoming the kind of parent you want to be today. Today is your new day and there is nothing impossible with God! He's not holding out on you. He will absolutely fulfill His Word. He is 100% faithful 100% of the time.

Notes

CHAPTER 5

THE STRATEGY OF *TENACIOUS FAITH*

The second strategy for entering into a season of breakthrough and living a life of sustained freedom is to develop tenacious faith. Tenacious faith doesn't rise and fall with every positive or negative circumstance—it holds fast to the fixed and stable promises of God with persistent resiliency. Once God has had the opportunity to develop tenacious faith in you, your emotions no longer rise and fall with every favorable or unfavorable thing that happens, and you're able to prevent what I call "roller coaster faith".

Roller coaster faith is the kind of faith that goes up and down, up and down, and all around. It's almost completely dependant upon present circumstances. Here's the scenario:

God speaks to you about your painful or upsetting situation and you're greatly encouraged. You're at the top of the roller coaster… high on adrenalin and stunning views. *Wheeeee! This is fun!*

Then symptoms or circumstances return with a jolt and you find yourself with a sinking feeling in the pit of your stomach. You begin to plummet down to the depths of despair. In your pain, fear, or panic you find it hard to even recall what God has said about your situation. The roller coaster is taking some sick twists and turns and you're feeling emotionally nauseous.

But God is faithful. He speaks to you about your situation again. He greatly encourages you, and once more you become joyful and confident in His word. Nothing is going to shake you this time because you're riding high on the coaster of faith! Ah yes, things may have gotten curvy, jerky, and dippy there for awhile—but you're convinced that those days are over and you're free from trouble now. The wind in your hair, the clarity of the view from the top, the exhilaration of knowing God's voice… you'll never fall for those "faith-stealing" demonic lies again!

That is, until your circumstances take a nosedive again, get bumpy again, get twisty and turny again—then you find yourself sinking into the depths of despair.

This cycle will make you double minded and bankrupt of any genuine faith. It's definitely a ride you want to get off! Why? (Other then the fact it's making you miserable). Because, even though God is faithful to continue to encourage you with His voice and His word—He wants you to *grow* in genuine, authentic, solid faith.

Here's a perfect example of "roller coaster faith", taken from the book of Exodus. While God was trying to free the children of Israel from the bondage of Egypt, they vacillated between faith, and doubt. Here's a short synopsis:

FAITH - God announces that soon there will be freedom from slavery in Egypt! The Israelites respond, "*And when they heard that the Lord was concerned about them and had seen their misery, they bowed down and worshiped.*"

DOUBT – But after Moses confronts Pharaoh, Pharaoh increases the Israelite's hard labor. The Israelites venomously say to Moses, "*May the Lord look upon you and judge you! You have made us a stench to Pharaoh and his officials and have put a sword in their hand to kill us.*"

FAITH – God spares the Israelites from the plague of death, and they leave Egypt in victory! The Bible tells us, "*The people bowed down and worshiped.*"

DOUBT – Uh oh… but then the Egyptians chase the Israelites to the Red Sea. The Israelites say to poor, beleaguered Moses, "*Was it because there were no graves in Egypt that you brought us to the desert to die?*"

FAITH – God parts the Red Sea and saves Israel! So, "*Miriam took a tambourine and all the women followed her with tambourines and dancing. 'Sing to the Lord for he is highly exalted.'*"

DOUBT – But then, the people get thirsty, so…: "*The people grumbled against Moses, saying 'What are we to drink?'*"

FAITH – God provides water and the Israelites are happy.

DOUBT – But then the Israelites get hungry in the desert and say to Moses (who has the patience of Job), "*you have brought us out into this desert to starve this entire assembly to death.*"

FAITH – God provides manna and the Israelites are happy.

DOUBT – But then, as they travel around in the desert, they get thirsty again. They say to Moses, "*Why did you bring us up out of Egypt to make us and our children die of thirst?*"

FAITH – God provides water and the Israelites are happy.

DOUBT – But then Moses stays a long time on Mt Sinai, so the Israelites tell Aaron to "*Come make us gods who will go before us. As for this fellow Moses who brought us up out of Egypt, we don't know what has happened to him.*"

The Israelites shifted from *faith* to *doubt* depending on how their circumstances looked. But it was God's design to use that situation to begin the work of building faith and trust in them. And it's the same with us. We may enter a trial with "roller coaster faith" (which is really just the pretense of faith, but won't hold together when the coaster hits the tracks), but if we allow God to do a full work in us, then we'll leave our trial with tenacious faith! We'll leave our trial mature, complete, and lacking nothing.

"*Consider it pure joy, my brothers, whenever you face trials of many kinds, because you know that the testing of your faith develops perseverance. Perseverance must finish its work so that you may be mature and complete, not lacking anything*." James 1:2-4

Our part is to fill up our hearts and minds with God's Word, learning to trust in His promises regardless of what our circumstances look like. His part is to build in us a tenacious faith which will not fail us in the years to come.

When God speaks to you—believe Him! Take Him at His Word. Write down the things He speaks and meditate on them morning, noon, and night. Keep them taped to your bathroom mirror or the refrigerator door. Keep His Word in front of your face until your trial has come to an end. You must hold on to the promises of God tenaciously. Be a spiritual pit bull. Clamp your jaw around those promises and don't let go until they are fulfilled. It may take a while, and you may have to make some changes in your life. It may take some repentance, and you'll definitely have to do things God's way. But eventually God's Word *will* come to pass.

*FULL*FILLMENT

In every miraculous breakthrough there's almost always a tempting "resting place" about halfway along the journey to the fulfillment of God's Word. It's the place where the Lord has completed "some" of what He's promised you, but not all. The place where it would be tempting to simply be appreciative for what God *has done* so far, rest on your laurels, and loiter for the rest of your life. A place where you cease to contend, press through, or exercise tenacious faith for the *full* manifestation of God's promise to you.

This is a dangerous place because, while sure… it's more comfortable and profitable then the place you initially began your breakthrough journey… it's not the place of *destiny*. The very nature of fulfillment is to be full. *Full* means: "Containing or holding as much or as many as possible; having no empty space; complete, whole, replete, entire, total." This Scripture in Psalm 57:2 says it perfectly: "*I cry out to God Most High, to God who will fulfill his purpose for me*." NLT

God doesn't do things halfway. What He spoke to you, He will accomplish. You don't need to "downgrade" your expectations to match your current experience. Your current experience is not an indication of what the future holds. God's Word is the indicator of what your future holds. What has *He* said to you? What has *He* told you to do? What has *He* promised you? That is what is true.

Once you've been in that "halfway resting place" for awhile, God will usually provide some *incentive* for you to keep moving. And by incentive I mean an uncomfortable circumstance or sticky situation. These things will remind you that this isn't your place of destiny. So keep truckin'.

For example, the FULLfillment of God's promise to me, as it related to the headache illness, was to receive freedom, preach freedom, and see others set free by God's power. However, my journey had several tempting resting places along the way, where it would have been easy to "camp":

- I could have permanently stopped at the radical blessing of not being dependant on painkillers anymore. That, in and of itself, was an absolute wonder to me! But I wanted more. I wanted full freedom and full healing from the headaches.
- Then, I could have stopped at the place where God spoke to me, "*No longer will any and every activity and stress have the power to give you a headache*." How wonderful to know that I could go on with my

life without the constant worry that every loud noise, bright light, or stressful occurrence would bring on a massive migraine. But I wanted and needed more. I wanted to be out of *all* pain, and I wanted to learn how to stand my ground.

- Then, I could have stopped at the place of rejoicing in my total healing and in my new-found ability to "stand" against the power and temptations of the enemy. I could have enjoyed my freedom privately and guarded the details of my upsetting trial carefully. But I wanted and needed more! I wanted to see others set free from the strongholds affecting *their* lives. I wanted others to learn how to stand their ground and walk in sustained freedom! Having tasted the joy of breakthrough, and having learned life-changing lessons—I wanted to fulfill my destiny to help set others free.

Here are a few scenarios of the "halfway resting place" from the Bible. I believe they'll inspire you to press through to the FULLfillment of what God has spoken to you:

- As a teenager, Joseph was promised great things by God. And at first it looked like everything was going his way. But in one day he went from being the favored son of his father to fighting for his life. Joseph was betrayed by his brothers, thrown into an empty well, taken captive by Midianite traders, and eventually sold into slavery. Oddly enough, things began to turn around for Joseph at this point. His master Potiphar was so impressed with him that he kept promoting Joseph until he was second in command in his master's house. This would have been an easy place for Joseph to settle down and "do life". He could marry… have kids… and enjoy the favor his position proffered him. But this wasn't his place of *destiny*. If you know the story, then you know Joseph's journey continued (with its ups and downs), until he ended up as second in command to Pharaoh himself. He was God's secret agent to save the entire Hebrew nation (not to mention all of Egypt) from famine! Had God allowed him to stay in Potiphar's house, he never would have fulfilled his *full* destiny. (Genesis 37–47)

- Hannah's God-given destiny was to be the mother of the great prophet Samuel. However, as a young woman, she found herself in adverse circumstances which definitely didn't predict this outcome. Hannah was married to Eli, who was also married to Peninnah. This made for an unhappy home life as Peninnah was able to have lots of babies, and Hannah was barren. However, Eli greatly preferred Hannah to Peninnah. Hannah could have savored and flaunted that love (just as Peninnah flaunted her ability to have children), and she could have been content to say, "*Maybe I can't have children, but my husband loves me the most!*" But Hannah wanted more. This was not her place of FULLfillment—and she pressed into God to receive her full desire. God heard her prayer and fulfilled her longing for children. (1 Samuel 1)
- Esther was a lovely young Jewish woman whose beauty gave her entrance into the palace of the King of Persia. And because of God's favor on her life, Esther was chosen as queen. When she received word that the Jews were to become the target of a violent and deadly attack, she rose up to save her people. Esther could have been content to enjoy the anonymity and safety her position provided, and let the Jewish people fend for themselves. But she was challenged by her uncle Mordecai to put her own life on the line and save the Jewish people. Her "resting place" of marriage, palace life, and favor, was just that, a resting place, not a place of permanency and fulfillment. (Esther 2-10)

In all these circumstances God provided the incentive to continue on the journey to FULLfillment. Many times, He un-feathers our nests, so to speak, so we'll get uncomfortable and make a *move*. Whatever promises God has made to you, one of your greatest challenges will be to press through until you see the fullness of that promise accomplished. Don't settle for halfway, because in doing so, you may miss your greatest achievements, accomplishments, and triumphs. Yes, it may be difficult to press through to fullness. Yes, it will take more courage than you personally possess. Yes, it may take patience. And it may involve some suffering, tears, and facing your worst fears. But it will be worth it! Press on to the FULLfillment of all God has spoken to you. Your life will never be the same.

NOTES

Chapter 6

Lessons about *Tenacious Faith*

Lesson 1: Developing Tenacious Faith is accomplished in Partnership with God. There is great freedom in knowing that developing tenacious faith is not your job alone. You are partnering with the Holy Spirit to grow and mature into the person He has called you to be. James 1:2-4 says it best: "*Consider it pure joy, my brothers, whenever you face trials of many kinds, because you know that the testing of your faith develops perseverance. Perseverance must finish its work so that you may be mature and complete, not lacking anything.*"

Persevering faith is not developed and matured *in spite of* tests and trials; it is developed *because of* tests and trials. Don't you agree that going through the ups and downs of life with Jesus by your side has made you resilient, long-suffering, and steady? But it's usually a private work between you and God… No one will ever know the depth of your private struggles. They'll never know the times you smiled when you wanted to cry, or praised when you wanted to panic. Nobody can see inside of your heart and know how hard it was for you to press through to God's promises. But HE knows. And He's building a testimony in you. He's building strength in you. He's building tenacious faith in you. You aren't who you used to be *because* you have pressed through your struggles, tears, panic, and fears! You are in process. You are a warrior.

God is always at work in us, and we are becoming more like Him little by little. And yet, isn't it frustrating when we become fearful and panicky at the first sign of trouble? I hate when I do that! For instance, several years ago my daughter was having a routine checkup at the pediatrician's office. As the doctor examined Amy's ear I could sense the energy in the room changing. (I was alarmed). She suggested we move into another examination room with different equipment so that she could take a more in-depth look. (I felt a stab of fear in my chest). She ended the appointment by telling me that Amy had a growth in her inner ear and would need to see a specialist right away. (I entered into full-blown panic!).

It turned out to be a fairly harmless osteoma (a benign bone growth) which was easily removed with minor surgery. Yes, it was a problem that needed attention—but it certainly wasn't the horrifying diagnosis I imagined it to be. So… why did I *fear* the worst as I stood in the pediatrician's examination room? Because my faith was still in the process of being developed and matured. And while I saw my reaction to this situation as a failure to trust God in the midst of an upsetting doctor's appointment, He saw it as the perfect time and place to continue to partner with me to bring about the maturation process.

Part of the maturation process involves learning to stop defaulting to "the worst case scenario." I'm sure you're familiar with the acronym for FEAR: False Evidence Appearing Real. But honestly, some of us are so jumpy we don't even need "false evidence" to get us imagining the worst case scenario. *Any* evidence will do… A hard month financially surely means bankruptcy is imminent. A grown child makes a dim-witted mistake, and we're just sure an orange jumpsuit is in their future. A week-long stomachache must be stage 4 cancer.

However, there's a better way to live if you'll yield to the Holy Spirit's work in your life. View your trials as the perfect greenhouse for God's continued work of building "tenacious faith" in you. Having said that, let me clarify that you definitely don't want to embrace or capitulate to your trial like it's your friend. It's not! Stand against sickness. Stand against pain. Stand against divorce, poverty, and addiction. But *yield* to the Lord. Yield your heart, your mind, your fears, your pain, and your bondage over to Him. He is the rescuer, the healer, and the redeemer!

It's in the midst of your trial and pain that God will do some of His finest work. Remember, in Romans 8:28 we read that God uses *all things* for the good of those who love Him (that's YOU!), and for those who are called according to His purposes (YOU again). He not only rescues you out of your trials, healing your body and restoring what was lost to you, He uses the hardships you've endured to make you tenacious and courageous.

Building strong faith is done in partnership with God!

Lesson 2: Faith Faces Forward. "*Forgetting what is behind and straining toward what is ahead, I press on toward the goal to win the prize for which God has called me heavenward in Christ Jesus.*" (Philippians 3:13b-14). A noteworthy characteristic of people who possess tenacious faith is an ability to face forward. They don't dwell on the past. They don't replay the traumas they've endured. They don't get stuck in the minutia of petty disagreements, gossip, or turmoil. They go forward and remain unconcerned about the insignificant details of yesterday, last week, or last year. They don't live with regrets. They repent when necessary, they apologize when it's appropriate, and they determinedly trek onward into their future. They have a clear grasp of what God has called them to, because they spend time in His Presence and they know His voice. These are the ones who receive breakthrough and walk in the fullness of it. No matter where you are on your journey today, this person can be *you*. Just face forward.

While there is a time and season in every life for healthy introspection (and maybe some inner healing sessions with a trusted counselor—especially as it relates to patterns of defeat) it becomes a problem when we *get stuck* looking backward.

I love a quote I recently came across from speaker and author Jeremy Pearson, as it perfectly explains what I'm discussing in this section:

"*In Jeremiah 29:11, the Lord says, 'For I know the thoughts and plans that I have for you'. We must go before Him and find out the plan, because that's what's on His mind. Plans belong to the future. You can't plan the past. So when God is thinking about you, He's not thinking about your past. And if He's not thinking about it, then why are you?*"

"*An unrelenting grasp on the past keeps people from walking in the thing God has called them, equipped them, graced them, and destined them to do. God isn't interested in talking about your past. He's waiting for you to start talking about what's on His mind: The plan. Your future.*"

"*We've become obsessed with our present position and current condition, when all the while He's trying to talk to us about our future. After God told Abram to leave his house, and he obeyed, then God told him to 'lift your eyes now and look from the place where you are—northward, southward, eastward, and westward; for all the land which you see I give to you and your descendants forever.*'" (Genesis 13:14-15)

"*This is the complete opposite of what most people do. They let down their eyes and look at where they are. But God told Abram, and He's telling you, 'Lift up and look from.' Instead of being obsessed with what you have or don't have or wish you didn't have, lift up your eyes and look from this place.*"

Lesson 3: Faith is a Journey. I live at the base of the Sierra Nevada Mountains and sometimes we go on day-trips to Yosemite. It's only about a three hour drive—but oh, what a drive! Huge climbs in altitude, followed by tons of twists and turns, concluding with an impressively long drop down into Yosemite Valley. If you'd never traveled to Yosemite from our home you might be tempted to wonder if you were on the right road. How is it that the Friedrichsen home is located at 4000 feet elevation—and Yosemite Valley is located at 4000 feet elevation—and yet we have to climb to over 8000 feet elevation during our journey? And why are there so many cliffs and twisty roads? Why do we travel so far north if, in fact, Yosemite is due west from our beginning point?

The journey might not make sense to you unless you had the map and knew the way.

Getting a sustained breakthrough is a lot like that. God takes you on a journey and there are many interesting twists and turns on the trip. Sometimes you'll feel like you're through the worst of it—when all of a sudden you find yourself going up, up, up another huge mountain. "*Hey? Wait a minute! We were going downhill... the worst was over... the best was ahead. How on earth did we end up climbing another huge mountain surrounded by a thick forest? This can't be right?*" Your temptation will be to try and figure out where you missed it (and sometimes you have missed it. If so, repent and get back on the right road).

Don't panic. Take a breath and remind yourself that you're not in the driver's seat. The Holy Spirit is, and He's been driving for quite some time. You needn't worry. You can trust Him. He's not going to pull over and idle awhile, just so you can languish in your panic, fear, or upset. He'll continue the journey. If it gets hot, or scary, or you get weary of going uphill, just hang on for a bit and soon you'll find yourself with different scenery. The Holy Spirit's job is to take you safely to your breakthrough. Your job is to trust.

As I journeyed through the trial of my headache illness, I taped the following Scripture on my kitchen cabinet and read it multiple times during the day: "*Blessed are those whose strength is in you, who have set their hearts on pilgrimage. As they pass through the Valley of Baca, they make it a place of springs; the autumn rains also cover it with pools. They go from strength to strength, till each appears before God in Zion.*" (Psalm 84:5-7)

When I studied this passage, I discovered that the phrase *Valley of Baca* means, "Valley of weeping in the desert" (boy could I relate!). Reading Psalm 84 reminded me that I was "passing through" my valley of weeping in the desert. My trial was not my new life, nor was it a permanent condition or a lasting location. I was "passing through"—and as I was, God was taking me from "strength to strength"! The key was to "set my heart on pilgrimage", even as I hung on for dear life.

Lesson 4: Scrutiny is Faith's Greatest Enemy. *Scrutiny* means: "searching examination or investigation; minute inquiry; surveillance; close and continuous watching."

Now, there are definitely some things worth scrutinizing. For instance, God's Word is something to be carefully examined and investigated. There is life in His Word, and the deeper you look, the more God will reveal to you! Also, God's Presence is a wonderful thing to scrutinize. Spend time in His Presence and He will take you deeper and deeper—showing you wonders about Himself. However, putting your current dilemma or crisis under a microscope and closely scrutinizing every detail and every angle will usually only lead to oppression. For example:

- If you're in the throws of an unhappy and difficult marriage, scrutiny will kill it. Picking apart every word or action your spouse says or does will only lead to more unhappiness and resentment.
- If you closely examine every tiny detail of your sickness, it will carry you deeper into pain and fear. As you meditate (which is what scrutiny is) on your pain, you will magnify it.
- If you obsessively scrutinize and think about your addiction, you will travel a dark road into further

bondage. You simply cannot solve your addiction problem by thinking about it over and over and over again.

- If you are constantly thinking about and scrutinizing your financial problems, you will end up in fear and despair, and be unable to sleep. Obviously there's a time to budget your funds and make a strategic financial plan. However, when you are drowning in debt and there isn't enough money to pay your bills, "thinking" about it and relentlessly turning it over and over in your mind won't solve the problem.

Over-thinking and over-scrutinizing your problem usually won't facilitate a solution. If it did, I would be the master of all solutions in life (and I wouldn't have to rely on the Holy Spirit for wisdom, insight, and peace). Compulsively scrutinizing your problems will lead to one destination: oppression. Not only that, after awhile it becomes a compulsion and you'll find yourself unable to stop, apart from an intervention from God.

If I've just described you, I have good news. Spending time in the Presence of God will help to deeply and profoundly wash your mind and spirit of the need to over-think your problems. Put on some worship music, lay on the floor, throw away your agenda and prayer list, and soak in God's Presence and love for a good long time. I assure you that after a week or two of *intentionally* spending time in His Presence each day, you'll be able to easily resist the compulsion to scrutinize your problems.

LESSON 5: PATIENCE IS FAITH'S GREATEST FRIEND. "*We do not want you to become lazy, but to imitate those who through **faith** and **patience** inherit what has been promised.*" (Hebrews 6:12, emphasis mine)

Faith and patience are a dynamic duo! Faith without patience will fizzle out when circumstances become trying. Patience without faith will "suffer well" but won't easily walk in the miraculous. But through faith *and* patience, you will inherit the promises of God.

Ten years ago, I stepped into a hole and injured my foot. This involved several visits to the orthopedic doctor, physical therapy, cortisone injections, and lots of ice packs. I'm an avid hiker, so you can imagine my disappointment at not being able to enjoy the activity I loved the most. This went on for a year and a half—and during that time I continually asked God to heal my foot.

About a year into the foot ordeal I attended a prayer meeting and asked the pastor to pray for my injury. He laid his hand on top of my foot and proceeded to ask God to *teach me a lesson.*

Seriously? That's the best you have for me? An innocuous prayer asking for…"a lesson"? Life is *full* of lessons, and God was indeed teaching me many lessons through that upsetting circumstance. But what I needed was healing.

I did my best to not lose heart and to hold on to the hope that my foot would be healed someday. Slowly but surely God developed faith and *patience* in me. I got to the point where I refused to change my hopeful outlook on the situation or to downgrade my expectations from God.

Without godly patience the following facts could have stolen my faith and robbed me of my breakthrough:

- The fact that my injury had gone on for so long.
- The negative prognosis of my doctor.
- The fact that the injury didn't show *any* signs of improvement, even with all the physical therapy, ice packs, and medical intervention.
- The fact that life seemed to be going on without me.
- The fact that even though I had stood in faith for the healing of my foot, I still hadn't experienced a breakthrough.

The foot story has a happy ending. One morning I was sitting on the couch reading a magazine about healing. As I read, I experienced what can only be described as a "gift of faith." I leapt off the couch and I *knew* I was healed! I called my prayer partner Lisa and told her what had happened. She said, "*Well, put on your shoes and go for a walk.*" And that's exactly what I did! I dusted off my walking shoes and went on a lovely, pain free walk. From that moment on my foot was totally, completely healed. Isn't God good!?

Faith without patience can lead to an unraveling of positive, godly works, and lead you to become double minded. For example, you stand your ground for weeks or months boldly declaring God's promise over your life—and you begin to experience hope and joy, and the first stages of breakthrough. Then, you get wearied by your trial, you get lied to by the enemy, and you get tempted to go back to the things God told you to leave behind. Momentum is lost, and breakthrough seems far away. While faith makes you able to hear and receive God's words of promise—patience keeps you *at that promise,* arms open, ready to receive. I have found that patience and hope are cohorts. Hope causes me to be joyful, because it assures me that the things God has spoken to me *will be* accomplished. And so, I get to live in the JOY of those promises even before they are fulfilled in the natural….all because I embraced patience. How cool is that?

"*Let us not become weary in doing good, for at the proper time we will reap a harvest if we do not give up.*" (Galatians 6:9)

Notes

Chapter 7

The Strategy of *Destiny Awareness*

The third strategy for entering into a season of breakthrough and living a life of sustained freedom is to identify and press into your destiny. Having an intentional, focused vision of your God-given destiny will aid in your pursuit of sustained freedom.

For example, God has called me to be a wife and mother. He has called me to be a teacher and communicator of His Word. He has called me to walk in vibrant good health and to enjoy my life. He has spoken specific promises to me regarding my future, which I am pressing into. I am a child of God, and I have a destiny! And because of this, I can't stand the thought of any obstacle, sin, or stumbling block diverting me. So, the awareness of my destiny helps me to sustain my breakthroughs and to resist going backwards.

What about you? What has God called you to? Do you have a desire in your heart that you just can't shake? If so, this may be "destiny awaking" in you. What has God been speaking to you about? Use the awareness of these prophetic words to help you resist staying in bondage.

When you find yourself afflicted, Destiny will raise her voice and cry, "*This isn't who I am! This isn't who I was meant to be! God has something better for me. This isn't my 'lot in life'! I'm better than this. My future is better than this!*"

- Destiny awareness will keep you on track when everything around you is trying to pull you away.
- Destiny awareness will push you, nag you, and drive you to experience breakthrough, so that you can fulfill God's purposes in your life.
- Destiny awareness will keep you living in "the promise" of your future dreams when you're in the midst of suffering. By doing so, it will keep you facing forward and pressing onward.
- Destiny awareness will help you remain obedient to the revealed will of God because you won't want to miss a moment of the wonderful life He has designed for you.
- Destiny awareness will cause you to sustain your breakthroughs. Going back to the old ways won't be an option if you have a clear focus of the beauty and purpose of the future God has planned for you.

"Squatters". . The Thief of Destiny

Let's imagine for a moment that you own a beautiful house in Florida. Although you don't currently live there, you have big plans for that lovely home someday. You've invested your life savings in renovating it and having it professionally decorated, and you've thoughtfully made it as comfortable as possible. Maybe your plan is to use it as a bed and breakfast cottage, or perhaps you plan to enjoy it as a vacation home for you and your extended family. It doesn't really matter the exact use you have in mind, the point is that it's *yours* and you have exciting plans for it.

In the course of time, a transient named Harvey notices that your lovely home is vacant. So he, his girlfriend, and his three dogs take up residence. They enter and exit the home by a basement door and remain unnoticed by the neighbors.

Reveling in his undetected comings and goings, Harvey invites his cousin, her teenaged son, and their cat to move in. The dogs aren't housebroken, the cat sprays, Harvey and his crew are slobs, and the house is being destroyed from the inside out. From the outside everything looks fine—but the inside of the house smells horrible and looks like a bomb went off.

You've got squatters on your property.

In the above example, the house is your destiny, and its essence is *you*. You are full of God's plans, promises, and purposes. Many of those plans and promises have yet to be fulfilled—but they're yours nonetheless. You've invested in your future in many ways, and you look forward with Spirit-inspired anticipation to all God has for you.

The "squatters" represent the demonic entities which try to "take up residence" in your life… stealing and spoiling your present and your future. Squatters invade the unattended or unguarded areas of your life. They seek to gain permanence and legitimacy by long-term residency. They not only wreak havoc on your current day-to-day life, they contaminate your destiny as well. And if left unattended, more will join them. Squatters are subversive in nature, and don't normally announce their arrival nor advertise their presence.

For example, the "squatter of addiction" didn't arrive at my front door and announce its intentions, "*Why, hello Paula. I'm here to devastate the next few years of your life, carry you into darkness, and ruin your credibility. My partner 'Hopelessness' will be joining us shortly.*"

No, addiction arrived on the heels of my propensity to over-medicate myself with prescription pain pills and sleep aids. But if you encountered me on the street during this time in my life you would have seen a normal looking woman… smiling and friendly. The bondage was *inside* the house, and could not be detected by a simple "drive by" encounter. My life was mired in affliction, and my destiny had been stalled. The squatters had taken over and I felt powerless, hopeless, despondent, and harassed.

Thankfully, squatters can be forced out and scared off of your property! A demonic squatter has no legal rights to afflict and torment you if you've been redeemed by Jesus Christ. However, unless you *know* and *act* upon that knowledge, you will remain bound. Four specific ways to deal with squatters are:

- Immerse yourself in God's Word.
- Immerse yourself in God's Presence.
- Deny the squatter entrance into your life (i.e. get help for addictions or compulsions, etc.)
- Take authority over the squatters until every last one has left (and get some anointed, powerful folks to help you evict the squatters, if need be).

Partnering with the Prophetic

It takes perseverance to enter a season of sustained breakthrough, and it takes "continued perseverance" to go one step further and press into your destiny. *Perseverance* means "steady persistence in a course of action, especially in spite of difficulties, obstacles, or discouragement." The way to adequately maintain the perseverance needed to press into all God has for you is by "partnering with the prophetic." Partnering with the prophetic involves hearing the Word of the Lord for your life—and then walking in faith, patience, preparation, and perseverance until that word is fulfilled. There's an interesting example of this scenario found in the book of Esther.

Wicked Haman had devised a murderous plan to annihilate the entire Jewish nation. Through the courageous actions of Esther and her uncle Mordecai, the plot was foiled. However, what I find interesting is the fact that King Xerxes' edict, "*granting the Jews the right to assemble and protect themselves*" was issued on "*the twenty-third day of the third month*"... yet the appointed day for this conflict wasn't until, "*the thirteenth day of the twelfth month*" (over seven months later!).

If you think about it, in reality the entire situation changed the moment the king wrote that edict. But the Jews didn't actually see the effect of that edict until many months later. The Jews had to "partner" with the King's word. First of all, they had to *believe* the word. Then they had to exercise *patience* for that word to come to pass. Next they had to *prepare* for the conflict even though it was many months away. And eventually they had to *persevere* against their enemies in the day of battle. In the end, they had to partner with the king's word to see it become their destiny.

And we must do the same. We are called to partner with the prophetic words the Holy Spirit gives us. We begin that partnership by pressing into our breakthrough and refusing to give up no matter what comes against us. *Destiny* is interwoven with *breakthrough*, and breakthrough will often precipitate destiny.

Here's what the sequence looks like when it comes to partnering with the prophetic:

- God speaks to you.
- God confirms His Word.
- It takes root in your heart and becomes an unshakeable thing which is dear to you.
- You begin to speak about it, pray about it, and plan for it.
- It is repeatedly substantiated in different ways.
- The enemy comes for it (which in-and-of itself is further substantiation of its validity).
- You fight for it with faith, patience, preparation, and perseverance.
- In the fighting for it, your dream and destiny are refined and defined—and the roots grow deep into your heart and mind.
- With deep roots, your dream and destiny are free to begin to flourish and thrive.

- You step into it! You won't be denied. You won't be swayed. Fear of man and fear of failure cannot stop you. It is yours!

I'm not sure where you are along that journey—but be encouraged that God rewards tenacity. He's seen you stand your ground when you have felt like giving up. He's seen you stay obedient to His directives, even when they didn't make sense to you. He's seen you continue to press into your destiny and calling, even when others put you down or doubted your ability to rise to the top. He's seen you persevere through unfathomable difficulties and hardship with a smile on your face and worship on your lips. Be encouraged that God sees and God knows—and He is a rewarder of those who diligently seek Him. Your new day is coming like the dawn! It's going to be bright and beautiful, and it's going to be worth each and every sacrifice you made along the way!

Notes

Chapter 8

Lessons about *Destiny Awareness*

Lesson 1 : Thanksgiving is Key to Walking in Destiny. Psalm 50:23 tells us, "*He who sacrifices thank offerings honors me, and he prepares the way so that I may show him the salvation of God.*" Every time I read this Scripture I think of a celebrity "red carpet" being rolled out for the Holy Spirit. The red carpet is our "thank offerings", and in a very literal sense, our thanksgiving paves the way for God to show us His salvation. (The Hebrew meaning of the word *salvation* in the Scripture above is: "Liberty, deliverance, prosperity, safety, open wide, and free.") The Lord *rides* in on the red carpet of our praise and thanksgiving to save, deliver, prosper, and free us! Our "thank offerings" are like a magnet, drawing toward us the salvation of God.

Let me give you two scenarios which have the same beginning but two very different endings to show you what I mean:

Scenario # 1 : You are a musician, and God has a call on your life. You've known for years that you're gifted to write songs, lead worship, and travel the world. God has confirmed this call many times, and those you trust have substantiated that you're very talented musically. And yet, you can't seem to catch a break.

Every time you try to get alone to song write, you end up distracted or pulled away by something else. The worship leader at church doesn't seem to notice you, even though you've dropped multiple hints that you're available. You've put the word out to other churches that you're willing to fill in at Sunday services or play for special events. You've had the chance to play at a few home group meetings—but other than that, every attempt you have made to "press into your call" has resulted in disappointment.

Over coffee with your musician friends, you complain pessimistically that nobody will give you a chance. You subtly criticize the worship leader at your church and delicately suggest that it seems to you that he only promotes and utilizes his friends on the worship team. You feel completely "overlooked" by anyone in authority, and struggle with self pity when it comes to breaking into the Christian music ministry and industry.

Little by little hopelessness sets in. You begin to feel that others are to blame that you haven't fully entered into your calling and God-given destiny. You feel like you're a victim of your circumstances and you wonder if you should possibly change churches, or even relocate entirely, in order to shake things up. You need God's intervention, favor, guidance, and some open doors.

You try, you strive, you complain. You. Are. Stuck.

Scenario #2: You are a musician, and God has a call on your life. You've known for years that you're gifted to write songs, lead worship, and travel the world. God has confirmed this call many times, and those you trust have substantiated that you're very talented musically. And yet, you can't seem to catch a break.

You realize something has to change. *You* have to change.

You dig deep into your relationship with God and you start pressing into His Presence. You rise early to worship

Him. You take long walks to have undisturbed fellowship with Him. You get into His Word like never before. You clear your schedule several times a week to develop your songwriting gifting. No phone calls, no texting, no Facebook….just you, your guitar, and Jesus. These things begin to stoke your creativity, and you find yourself singing prophetically over the stagnant areas of your life. The more you press into worship, the more the fountain of living-water-worship seems to flow from within you. You are captured by His love, by His personality, by His beauty, and it is changing you. Songs of life are flowing out of you! You are changing the atmosphere of your family, your workplace, and your church! Something wonderful is going on with you and people are beginning to take notice.

Slowly doors of opportunity begin to open to you, and little by little you enter into your call. Gone are the dreams of grandeur and your hope of being an overnight success. Those childish wishes have been replaced by a servant's heart and a deep well of thanksgiving and worship. You have become enamored with the atmosphere of heaven and you are no longer content to be mired in the petty, insignificant, and base things of life. You live for the days when you can carve out hours to spend in communion with the King of Kings.

* * *

That, my friend, is an example of what Psalm 50:23 means by "sacrificing thank offerings". It's a heartfelt, unrushed, intimate, wholehearted, persistent flow of praise and thanks! It's the red carpet the Holy Spirit rides in on to bring *salvation* (liberty, deliverance, prosperity, safety, and freedom).

I'm pretty sure that the sound of thanks and praise is like fingernails on a chalkboard to Satan. It sends him fleeing! As you make the choice to refuse to complain, gossip, or grumble when faced with difficulty or closed doors, you've taken an important first step toward your "salvation". But don't stop there! Begin to confess and declare the greatness of

God over your situation. Begin to sing prophetically over your unruly circumstances. As you do, you create a welcome red carpet environment for the Holy Spirit. And when the Holy Spirit arrives on the scene, everything changes. He's the most loving, supportive, nurturing, funny, winsome, brilliant celebrity in the universe!

Lesson 2: Destiny Won't Always be Comfortable. Sometimes being in your comfort zone can feel like peace—but it's not true peace. True peace is experienced as you stay in step with the Holy Spirit. I can be tempted to believe true peace is found relaxing on the couch watching Food Network, or in my predicable role as a housewife, or in my part time job at my church. After all, nobody challenges or criticizes me in these familiar roles.... I'm *comfortable*. However, if I snuggle too long in these places of comfort and familiarity I begin to sense a feeling of regret niggling at me. Why? Because I know I was made for more than this! I have dreams and creativity simmering in me. To stay in this place of "pseudo peace" eventually leads to anxiety.

And so...I must press on into my destiny. I must get busy. The day I began writing this book I posted the following status on my Facebook page: "*Killing some giants today. It's gotta be done in order for me to enter fully into my exciting, fulfilling future. It's so much easier to discuss the promises God has given me, to strategize about the promises, journal about the promises, and dream about the promises. But the actual killing of the giants, facing my fears, doing the hard work, and pushing through demonic bullies to ENTER into my promises, is far more difficult!*"

I bet you can relate. I'm sure I'm not the only one who finds it far easier to "strategize" about my promises then to actually commence the hard work of *doing* what God has called me to do. If given the choice between meeting friends at Starbucks to discuss writing a book about the subject of "breakthrough" or actually sitting in my office alone for hours writing the book, I'd take the former. It's hard work *entering* into the new thing God has called you to do! However, without the hard work, it's unlikely you'll enter in.

Even though I write often, it still takes me out of my comfort zone each time I embark on a new project. It's still a risk. I still have to face off with the "fear" that I won't have anything of worth to say. Fear that my words won't be relevant. Fear that I won't succeed. But without risk, life is distilled down to safe, predictable, and unsurprising. As the famous quote says, "Every accomplishment starts with the decision to try."

I like what author and speaker Kevin Dedmon has to say about risk: "*Most people do not take risk because they lack confidence that God will come through on His end of the partnership and intervene in our risk-taking efforts. As believers, it is essential that we understand that God is faithful; when we take risk, He comes. If we truly believe God is able to do the impossible then, like Abraham, we will determine to ride upon the prophetic promises that God has given us to carry out. We will live in the hope that God is faithful to provide what we need to bring about the promise that our risk is releasing. We can only enter into our God-given supernatural destiny as we step out in risk.*" (Risk Factor by Kevin & Chad Dedmon)

Lesson 3: Resistance Builds Muscle. In previous chapters I discussed the fact that to experience "sustained breakthroughs" you will have to *grow in spiritual strength* and learn to persevere. But here's the good news: God has been building spiritual strength in you *for* your destiny. Resistance builds muscle. Without spiritual muscle you may lack the stamina to endure long-term in your calling. Here is what a lack of spiritual stamina looks like:

- You begin an important project filled with passion, creativity, and inspiration—only to buckle when the enemy "pushes back" on your dream. As soon as the fire gets turned up, you bail. You simply do not have the spiritual muscle to hold your ground. You get shoved around by the enemy, and pretty soon you're saying things like, "*I just don't feel peace on this project right now. Maybe I'll continue later.*"

- You begin an important project filled with passion, creativity, and inspiration—only to fall into major sin when the enemy tempts you. Going forward into your destiny will pique the interest of the enemy's camp, so unless you are "strong in the Lord and in the power of His might", you will surely find yourself in over your head. This is why the Lord so carefully and patiently works strength in you during your tests and trials *before* you enter fully into your calling. If you've been going through some very intense trials, you can rest assured that God will use them for your good! God is shaping and molding you in the midst of your difficulties and giving you spiritual vigor. Just like lifting weights is taxing on your physical body—building spiritual muscle is taxing too. But, oh it's worth it in the end! It's worth it when you begin to walk in the promises of God! It's worth it when you see your dreams fulfilled! What has cost you much now will reap huge rewards later. So hang in there. Don't give up. Keep walking through your trial until you're on the other side, because the "other side" is glorious!

Christian Life Coach Martin Flack says, "*Your greatest ministry effectiveness will come out of the areas God has most deeply shaped you.*" In other words, sometimes it's the very worst places of weakness, vulnerability, sin, failure, or grief which can be the most powerful areas of future ministry for you. Personally, I've found that the *very* weapon the enemy threatens me with, is often the *very* weapon I've used to later assault his realm.

We see this principle worked out in 1 Samuel 17 in the familiar story of David and Goliath. Goliath—who was nine-feet-of-ugly—came toward David dressed in a bronze helmet, a coat of armor, bronze greaves on his legs, a javelin slung on his back, carrying a sixteen pound iron spear, and a sword strapped to his side. And, oh yeah… he also had a shield bearer to walk in front of him…just in case.

As Goliath reached David for the "big battle", he scoffed at the handsome young man, dressed only in normal clothing. He couldn't believe he'd been reduced to fighting a teenager with a slingshot. And so Goliath did what all demonic bullies do—he prophesied doom over David. He said, "*Am I a dog, that you come at me with sticks? Come here, and I'll give your flesh to the birds of the air and the beasts of the field*!"

David ran toward Goliath and prophesied right back at him, "*You come against me with sword and spear and javelin, but I come against you in the name of the Lord Almighty, the God of the armies of Israel, whom you have defied. This day the Lord will hand you over to me, and I'll strike you down and cut off your head*."

As we all know, David did kill Goliath with one smooth stone to the forehead (which was basically the only unprotected spot on Goliath's body). However, look what happened next. David walked up to Goliath, drew Goliath's own sword, and cut off his head—just as he said he would. David used the *very weapon* his enemy had threatened him with, to cut off the source of lies, threats, and demonic boasting.

And it's the same with us. Our places of weakness and attack can give us entrance into our destiny, if we allow God to shape, correct, and strengthen us. The very places where the enemy has previously threatened you and prophesied weakness, inability, failure, or death—are the very places you can now succeed, thrive, minister, and triumph!

Author and teacher Graham Cooke says, "*If we have a giant in our life it is because we are meant to be a giant ourselves. The circumstances in front of us are designed to increase our size in the Spirit. So upgrade your stature in relation to Jesus and radically increase your power in the*

Holy Spirit. Or, if you prefer, just quit and never realize your true self and the inheritance that goes with it."

When I was in the thick darkness of chronic pain and narcotic dependency, the Lord spoke Isaiah 35:1 as a promise to encourage me: "*The desert and the parched land will be glad; the wilderness will rejoice and blossom.*"

I asked the Lord, "*What does it mean that the desert will bloom and rejoice?*" He said, "*It means that the place of your greatest desolation will become the greatest place of the manifestation of My glory.*" And, oh man, was this ever true! The place of my greatest darkness, pain, and testing, became the place where God repeatedly manifested His glory in my life…the glory of His healing and deliverance, of His comfort and of His Presence.

What has God called you to? Use the awareness of those prophetic promises to help propel you past your pain and into your purpose. Destiny is worth fighting for!

Notes

Chapter 9

The Strategy of *Transforming Love*

The fourth strategy for entering into a season of breakthrough and living a life of sustained freedom is to encounter, engage, and be transformed by the love of God. The love of God is displayed and proclaimed throughout the whole universe, and it is demonstrated in the beauty and intricacy of life and creation. And yet, *observing* the love of God is not the same as *having* an intimate, transforming, ongoing encounter with the love of God.

Some people feel as though they are observing the love of God through a large picture window. They clearly see His love. They sing worship songs about His love. They tell others about His love. They have a correct Biblical theology about His love. And, at times, they experience the warmth of His love through that picture window. However, they haven't yet broken through to the place of *intimacy* and *encounter* when it comes to His love.

The Holy Spirit wants to break through our barriers and fill us with His Presence and His love. And I don't mean in an ethereal or vague kind of way, but in a solid, tangible, transforming kind of way. God's aim is to so fill us with His Presence that we become immersed in an achingly exquisite, life changing exchange with Him. An exchange that so transforms our life that it becomes a flourishing, thriving, joyous adventure.

Healing the "Badlands" of Our Soul

God wants to bring a river of His Presence into the "Badlands" of your life. The Badlands are the places that are "heavily eroded, difficult to traverse, uncultivable, and barren". What are your Badlands? What has become eroded in your life? What has become uncultivable and unfruitful? There isn't any area of your life that an ongoing encounter with the Presence of God can't transform!

When my son was just two years old, I noticed that I would become unreasonably angry at him during the course of each day. Any little thing could set me off. I remember actually experiencing a burning feeling in my chest when I'd get irritated with him. This went on for a couple of months and I recall thinking that I couldn't raise my precious son without receiving healing for this issue immediately. So I sought the Lord. Like irrigating dry, unproductive land, God's Presence began to flood into my heart, mind, and soul, filling me with His love. Slowly but surely the power of the Holy Spirit broke that spirit of anger and restored a peaceful mother's heart to me. Yes, I still got irritated and angry with my son at times—but the "unreasonable burning anger" was gone. Yet, you must know, my breakthrough didn't come because I exerted my will to stop overreacting. I stopped burning with anger over the antics of my two year old because I had encountered God's Presence and He was filling the Badlands of my soul with His joy and love. He was transforming me from the inside out!

Up Close and Personal

Our relationship with God was never supposed to be a *far away* experience. Sometimes we get stuck in the trap of thinking we need to "get it together" before we come too close to God. Like maybe He'll be repulsed by our humanity and reject us. We worry that He's displeased with us because we're struggling with the Badlands of our lives. We think if we could just find someone who has a "close up" relationship with God to pray for us, *then* we would be healed, delivered, and get a breakthrough (and actually, asking an anointed believer to pray for us is always a good thing to do!). We wonder how to close the gap and draw near to God?

It is so easy to close the gap between you and God that you will be stunned—**simply spend time with Him**. James 4:8 tells us, "*Come near to God and he will come near to you.*" Jeremiah 29:13 says, "*You will seek me and find me when you seek me with all your heart.*" You might hesitate to simply "draw near to God" when you are so aware of the unruly Badlands in your life… the areas of sin, or failure, or barrenness. But here's the crux: it's God's job to flood the Badlands, thereby changing your nature—it's your job to draw close to Him and spend time with Him so He can easily access your heart and mind.

When I was a young girl, I had a little Catholic booklet about "saints." I remember being enthralled with the lives of these godly people and their great exploits for Jesus. Yet, oddly enough, each time I would read the book I would feel far away from God. You see, although I was inspired by the holiness of these remarkable saints—their "goodness" only seemed to magnify my own inability to "be good". So reading it made me inwardly shy away from God because it highlighted a sense of unworthiness in me.

You can't imagine my relief many years later when I discovered that it was by the blood sacrifice of Jesus Christ, and in fellowship with the Holy Spirit, that I could act, think, and *be* holy. This truly was good news for me! What joy to find out Jesus was fully able to "*sympathize with my weaknesses because He had been tempted in every way—yet was without sin.*" There was such freedom in the knowledge that I could run full throttle to His "*throne of grace with confidence, so that I could receive mercy and find grace to help me in my time of need!*" (Hebrews 4:15-16)

For example, if I had avoided the "throne of grace" when I was dealing with the burning anger issue toward my two-year old, the anger would have escalated. I couldn't "fix" myself before I came into God's Presence. It was only God who could bring me deliverance from anger. Coming into His Presence gives me access to what He offers me and ushers me into a reciprocal love relationship. It's like this:

- He offers correction—I offer repentance
- He offers wisdom—I offer joyful obedience
- He offers fellowship—I offer time
- He offers His Presence—I offer my worship
- He offers conversation and laughter—I offer conversation and laughter
- He offers love—I offer love

Love for Love's Sake Alone

While my need for breakthrough drives me closer to the Presence of God, it is *love for love's sake alone* which keeps me close to Him. Yes, I desire to walk in sustained freedom and breakthrough for the rest of my life—but God's Presence is so compelling, so delightful, so enthralling, so remarkable, so beguiling, and so resplendent, that it is reason enough to devote time to Him each day. And certainly, I don't leave His Presence when that "devoted" time is over. I go through my day "sodden" with His Presence and cognizant of His companionship.

Don't let your failures, sins, mistakes, and sense of unworthiness hold you back from your Abba Daddy one minute longer. He loves you! He hasn't given up on you. He has a plan to release you from your darkness, and His plan will unfold as you spend time in His Presence. But the deliverance, healing, and wholeness that you'll receive in His Presence are just the first-fruits of time spent with God. It is *love for love's sake alone* that we seek Him, for He is worthy.

Awakened to Your New Season

God has a season of breakthrough for you, and it's closer than you think…

On a chilly day in late March, I was on my daily walk. I had on thick sweat pants, two sweatshirts, mittens, and a wool beanie. The wind was biting cold and snow flurries swirled around me as I walked. The sky was gray, the fields were brown, the birds were silent, and the world around me was quiet and dormant. The weather seemed to match my temperament that day. As the cold breeze sliced through me, I zipped my sweatshirt as high as it would go and pressed on, "enduring" my walk. It was then that God spoke to me, "*Paula, if you aren't observant you'll miss the signs that spring has arrived.*"

Hmm…. It sure didn't seem to me like spring had arrived. But I slowed down and began to look around. I had been so busy stoically "soldiering" on through my daily walk (and my daily life), I hadn't even been aware that my surroundings *had* subtly changed. Sure enough, tender blades of green grass were beginning to poke through the cold ground. There was less snow on the local mountains. The trees had leaf clusters which were just days from emerging. Signs of spring were everywhere. I had simply failed to notice them! And I believe *your* springtime has arrived and that you're entering into a new season of *intimacy* and *encounter* with the Presence of God, like you've never before experienced!

Our lives are an ongoing journey of nearness to God. As we draw near we behold new facets, angles, and perspectives of His personality and beauty. The deeper we immerse ourselves into companionship, friendship, and "oneness" with Him, the more we are filled and transformed. This transformation is our springtime! It is a time of beauty and new beginnings… A time of flowers, fragrance, and singing… It is a time of healing and renewal… And a time to come out of your "winter of affliction" and dance with God again.

He is calling you deeper. He is calling you nearer. He is calling you to Himself, to love, to laughter, to holiness, and to romance. Are you ready to respond?

"*My lover spoke and said to me,*
"Arise, my darling,
my beautiful one, and come with me.
See! The winter is past;
the rains are over and gone.
Flowers appear on the earth;
the season of singing has come,
the cooing of doves
is heard in our land.
The fig tree forms its early fruit;
the blossoming vines spread their fragrance.
Arise, come, my darling;
my beautiful one, come with me."
(Song of Songs 2:10-13)

Notes

Chapter 10

Lessons about *Transforming Love*

Lesson 1: Three's a Crowd. You were made for intimacy and designed for love. At the heart of every person is the need to love and be loved. And while human love goes a long way in satisfying this desire, our hearts will *never* be fully satisfied apart from a romance with our Creator. We were wired to know God, to love Him, and to walk and talk with Him in the garden of intimacy.

However, if we're constantly surrounded with people, noise, activities, and events, then we're actually "shielding" ourselves from intimacy with God. For example, if my husband Jeff and I are never alone together, how can we continue to build our friendship and romance? If Jeff always wanted others around, I would wonder if he was using people and activity as a buffer between the two of us. And it's the same in our relationship with God. We need time alone with Him.

That's not to say that some of us aren't wired to love being around lots of people. If you're a "people person" then you just naturally get revived and energized by being around others. This is completely legitimate, and it's who you are. But you'll still need to carve out quality quiet time to be alone with God if you're going to be intentional about deepening your love-relationship with Him. Having a meaningful encounter with the Holy Spirit in a group meeting is just as valid as having a meaningful encounter with the Holy Spirit alone on your living room floor. The only difference is the latter was provoked by an intentional pursuit of God based on your passionate desire for His Presence! This kind of seeking will greatly enhance your private story with Him.

If my husband only showed me affection when we were in a large group of people, I would be disappointed. I would wonder if he was putting his arm around me or giving me a hug to impress those around us, as if to say, "*Look at me; I'm such a wonderful, loving husband!*" His affection would still be appreciated, but it might lack depth. As a wife, I welcome my husband's hugs, kisses, loving words, and smiles most of all when we're alone.

This example correlates to our relationship with God. While our corporate times of worship are vibrant and joyous—helping us to explore the deep recesses of God's love and personality together—it can't replace a meaningful, vibrant, *private* relationship with God. Enjoying my husband's company at a dinner party, his arm draped over my shoulder, laughing together with our friends—cannot replace sitting in the swing chair in our backyard, under our enormous shade tree, sharing a cold drink, and talking about our day together. In fact, our marriage is *built* on our private times together.

To live a life of sustained breakthrough you'll need to become intentional about pursuing God's Presence in your everyday life. And for those of us who come alive being around large groups of people, this may require discipline. But the price is worth the payoff! According to Hebrews 11:6 "*God rewards those who earnestly seek Him.*" The word *earnestly* means, "serious in intention, purpose, or effort."

When I was experiencing my chronic headaches, I briefly got in the habit of lying on the couch and watching TV for hours at a time. I wanted to forget my problem and I was seeking relief in inane reality TV shows. And to be honest, watching brainless television shows did bring me some relief (I dare you to obsess over your problems while watching The Real Housewives of Beverly Hills). However, it also robbed me of my earnestness. Each day it got easier to drift away from my pattern of earnestly seeking God. Each day it got easier to hide in my prescription drug haze, watch Bravo TV, and blandly hope for a better tomorrow. Each day I became a bit more disconnected from the passionate, proactive Christ-follower I had always been.

Although I was no longer intentionally pursuing God during my several month escapade into the cesspool of daytime reality TV, He continued to pursue me! He comforted me and helped me. But (and hear me on this point), there was no "reward." Remember, the Scripture I quoted above says, "*God rewards those who earnestly seek Him.*" The greatest reward we can ever hope to receive is His Presence, because He is the most winsome, glorious, gorgeous person in heaven and earth! His Presence is also the best "reward" because *everything* good in our lives—healing, joy, prosperity, peace, restoration, righteousness, and deliverance—is found *in* Him. So, the reward for seeking Him is always Him.

In my TV watching stupor, I was like a car running on empty. Yes, God would graciously give me enough gas to get through each day—but I was never overflowing. I didn't have anything to offer anyone else, as I was pretty much bankrupt of His Presence myself.

If you broke down the anatomy of my deliverance from the headache illness and the pain medication dependence, you would be able to trace the starting point back to one thing… an intentional pursuit of God's Presence. As I mentioned at the beginning of this book, this renewal of my passion for God came through my dear friend Jim DeGolyer. And I guess I want to "pay it forward." I want to stimulate in you a desire to begin to spend time in God's Presence in a deeper and more deliberate way. I want to whet your appetite for the wonders He has waiting for you in that place of undisturbed devotion. Because it'll blow your mind, and you'll never be the same!

Lesson 2: Born to Soar. You were born to soar on eagle's wings. You were created to circle the Son, allowing the radiance of His glory to reflect off your wings. You were designed to wait in His Presence, receive His strength, and glide on the currents of His affection.

Isaiah 40:31 says, "*But they that wait upon the Lord shall renew their strength; they shall mount up with wings as eagles…*" The Hebrew meaning of the word *wait* is, "to expect, to tarry, to bind together as by twisting." When I think about "binding together as by twisting" I think of intimacy and being face to face with the One who is inextricably intertwined in my life. This is so much more than our usual definition of the word "wait" in this Scripture:

- Some people think that the word "wait" in Isa. 40:31 is praying a rehearsed list of requests during their devotion time each day.
- Some people teach that the word "wait" in Isa. 40:31 means that we are to wait on God like a "waiter" waits on a table in a restaurant. We gather His requests and then do our best to fill the order (as if the objective of our time with Him is to "get our marching orders")
- Some people believe that the word "wait" in Isa. 40:31 means to sit in stone silence until they hear a "Word from God." Each day is sort of a dice roll on whether or not God will speak to them.

However, when we understand the word "wait" in light of the original Hebrew definition, it burgeons with meaning. Remember, it means "to expect, to tarry, to bind together as by twisting."

- Waiting upon the Lord is tarrying unhurriedly in His Presence. *Tarry* means to "to remain or stay, sojourn; to linger; to loiter."
- Waiting upon the Lord is an open, honest exchange. You are "bound together as by twisting" with Him, and He knows everything about you. Allow that knowledge

to pull down any perceived barriers and *be real with Him*.

- Waiting upon the Lord is lying on the floor; arms flung wide, allowing His Presence to flow into the Badlands of your life. No agenda. No list. No requests. No regrets.
- Waiting upon the Lord is taking walks with Him, enjoying the beauty around you, talking, laughing, joking, and listening.
- Waiting upon the Lord is drinking in His Word in a secluded place, and allowing that Word to seep deep into your heart, comforting and challenging you.
- Waiting upon the Lord is sitting in a heap and crying. He's not repelled by your grief. He's not alarmed by your sadness. He draws near to you even when the most you can do is cry. Crying can be a prayer in-and-of-itself when done in the Lord's Presence.
- Waiting on the Lord is worshiping Him exuberantly in your car on the way to work—or playing the guitar for hours in your room while you draw near in private praise.
- Waiting upon the Lord is being unabashedly hopeful that He's going to move supernaturally in your difficult situation. Like a child who looks up into Father's face expectantly—you are waiting on your Abba Father. You are eager, expectant, and hopeful! Nothing can shake your faith because you've spent so much time in His Presence. You know Him… and you know He is faithful.

Lesson 3: Marinated in His Presence. Our wounds should compel us to seek the Healer. God never intended that we handle our problems on our own; instead He wants our distress to move us deeper into His Presence.

When meat is marinated, it's the pierced areas which soak up the liquid. As we immerse ourselves in God's transforming love, it's the pierced parts of our lives which draw in the healing waters of His Presence. This is why breakthrough so often follows a radical increase of *intimacy* and *encounter* with the Presence of God. The places of woundedness come into proximity with the living water of the living God and everything changes! The living water brings transformation. The living water yields holiness, boldness, joy, restoration, character formation, peace, and healing! When you marinate in His Presence, the pierced places of your life become whole—and your ability to sustain breakthrough increases exponentially.

Your Time has Come!

I believe the fact that you're reading this book right now is a prophetic indication that *your* time of breakthrough has come! This is your "Baal Perazim" (the place of breakthrough). Nothing can shake you, and nothing can take you from this place of freedom in your life. You rest securely against the breast of Jesus…in a concealed place of friendship, intimacy, and privilege. A place where your "breakthrough" is just the starting point—and where you have discovered that *encounter* and *intimacy* with the Presence of God is the aim of it all (and the *real* starting place for the rest of your life).

"I am my lover's and he is mine…"
Song of Songs 6:3

Notes

About the Author

Paula Friedrichsen speaks at women's retreats and church conferences regionally as well as nationally.

Paula began writing professionally in 2004, and saw her first book, "*The Man You Always Wanted is the One You Already Have*" (Multnomah) published in January 2007.

Jeff and Paula have been married since 1984 and are the proud parents of two young adults. Jeff also has two grown daughters and five terrific grandkids.

You can find out more about Paula's ministry at www.PFMinistries.com or you can email her at Paulafriedrichsen@live.com

Made in the USA
San Bernardino, CA
28 June 2014